Tell Me 'Bout the Good Old Days

Text by
KEN TATE

Paintings by
JOHN SLOBODNIK

HOUSE of
WHITE
BIRCHES

Grandpa, tell me 'bout the good old days." Daniel and I were walking, hand in hand, on the old home place; his request was the same I had made of my own Grandpa Tate many years before.

In an instant, I was a youngster again, begging Grandpa to share another story of the magical time he always called "the Good Old Days."

What is it about grandpas and their stories that capture the imagination of youngsters? Fish caught are always bigger, bullies fought always meaner and lessons taught always truer.

I looked up to Grandpa Tate, measuring my stature against his character just as he measured me against the old barn wall. Eyeing me up and down, he opined: "I do believe this boy's grown a foot in the last year!" If Grandpa said it, it *must* be true. So I pulled in a deep breath, stood as straight as I could and maybe even cheated, pushing up on tiptoes—just a little—to measure up to Grandpa's expectations.

And so it goes in life. It wasn't that many years until I was measuring the years of my own son against the door frame leading to his bedroom. Those marks are still there, lacquered over, but indelibly grooved into the board. Now I look forward to Daniel's marks on another measuring board.

"Grandpa, tell me 'bout … ." I guess that is one way I have of sharing with Daniel—and you—some of the vignettes that made up the measuring board of life for so many of us back in that time called the Good Old Days.

John Slobodnik

We always seemed to sense when the last snow of the winter had fallen. Often it covered the crocuses and jonquils like a thick, white, woolen coat. Trees already were cast with the hue of the approaching spring.

March snows in our neck of the woods were known to be among the heaviest, so my sister and I took advantage of the fluffy stuff to roll up one more snowman. But as sure as a crocus or jonquil will recover from its tent of white, Frosty had a dim future in the bright sunlight and lengthening days.

It was a bittersweet moment for two youngsters. Another season of youth melted away, and we were left with soggy scarf, drooping carrot and hard, hard coal. But in its place was the awakening wonder of blooms and spring peepers and the first robin of the new season!

How long could childish lament continue for a melted companion with the approach of kite-flying season and the promise of barefoot days ahead?

When I see the kite kits sold in stores today, I'm at once envious and sad. Back in the Good Old Days, we had no choice but to make our own. No plastic sheeting or tempered skeleton. No synthetic string.

I wish I could take you back with me. In my mind's eye I see Grandpa or Daddy helping us construct a cross and frame of balsawood. Newspaper became our wings, glued taut to the frame. To balance the kite, keeping it steady in the winds of March, we tied on a tail made from a strip of Mama's worn-out gingham dress and festooned with bows of quilting scraps. We had to fly trial after trial, cutting away or adding ballast until the weight was right.

Then we were airborne! Few of us in those olden days ever got the chance to fly, but our magic carpet was our kite. Our blue-sky fantasy was bound only by the length of our ball of twine.

Yes, it's easier to get today's kites constructed and joyfully bouncing in the March wind. But I wouldn't exchange one moment of our construction time with Daddy and Grandpa for all the plastic kites in the world!

John Slobodnik

*T*he winds of March subsided, April showers prevailed and the rituals of spring began. Life was a lot slower in the Good Old Days, or at least that's the way it seemed, so we had more time to notice the movement of those rituals through our lives.

A case in point would be a soggy drive down a country lane. The cars were slower, but that was fine, since the track was slower, too. "Puddlejumpers"—that's what we called the cars back then, and for good reason! Jumping puddles and slipping down mud ruts in our old flivver, we youngsters giggled with glee from the backseat.

In those slower days, we could stop and let Mama Duck waddle her brood across the road. "One, two, three, four, five!" we called out, pretending they were boxcars passing at a railroad crossing. The only air conditioning was a rolled-down window or dropped isinglass curtain, so we could feel the sweet spring breeze, its rain-cleansed scent mingled with the earthiness of the dirt road and the passing farm fields.

Think of all we miss in today's world as we zoom by on freeways and interstate highways! Give me the road less traveled, the old puddlejumper and the cleansing of a warm April shower.

John Slobodnik

*B*ack in the Good Old Days, we had to make our own fun. There were no video games, computers or televisions to take up our time. And there would have been plenty to do around the farm if I had uttered the words, "I'm bored!"

So it was that we found plenty to fill our days. Most of it was free for the taking in the great playground outside the bounds of our tiny home.

There I hunted creek beds for arrowheads.

There my friends and I dug out foxholes and made forts and acted out heroic wartime exploits that we had heard about on the radio or had seen on the newsreels at the movie theater.

There we ran, unfettered by the constraints of adulthood through woods, pastures and hollows.

And what if a picnic for doll and dog, complete with cookies and milk, were intruded upon by a sudden April shower? Why, just raise the umbrella and wait for that cloud to pass. The mud pies that would follow were all part of making our own fun back in the Good Old Days.

$\mathcal{T}$here was no need to worry about lint in the dryer back when I was a youngster. Our dryer was energy-efficient and ecologically pure. That dryer was the clothesline, stretched from a huge oak tree to a cedar-post T to the west of our home.

Is there any perfume sweeter than the scent of clothes dried by a gentle May breeze? How we kids loved to drift off to sleep snuggled between quilts and sheets that still billowed with that softness. Today's laundry products can only hope to imitate what we took for granted. Daddy's longhandles and Mama's unmentionables adorned the line along with mundane shirts, overalls, blouses and dresses.

No May—or Mother's Day—goes by without my mind filling with the picture of Mama's hands pinning up line after line of laundry. Those same hands pieced that quilt, sewed and hemmed that skirt, patched that hole in the knee of my best pair of Big Smiths. They also mended cuts, bruises and hurt feelings with the same love and motherly efficiency. Clothes on the line or tear-stained cheeks—Mama saw to it that everything was clean and dry.

$\mathcal{M}$ama was, as were millions of other mothers like her, the supreme example of sacrifice to little boys like me. "Man may work from asun to sun, but a woman's work is never done." Mama was the absolute embodiment of the old adage.

A large garden always fed our family, so we were not strangers to pulling God's goodness from the soil. Mama worked tirelessly in the rows, growing tomatoes, beans, corn and cucumbers to can, dry, pickle and preserve. She also led us on berry-picking forays, fighting off ticks and chiggers to make sure her jam and jelly was cooked up for the coming year. What was started by the light of day she often finished by the lamp of night. To say she worked like a man would be an insult. Mama worked like a woman!

Sometimes I think Mama believed that good kids were raised much like a good garden. If you put in enough hard work and perseverance, planting in good soil and relying on providential rain in due season, you will ultimately reap what you sow.

Whether in garden or life, I have tried to follow the lessons of sacrifice and selflessness Mama taught me back in the Good Old Days.

$\mathcal{J}$anice and I had known each other for four months before I worked up the courage to ask her for a date. We attended neighboring schools and had been introduced by a mutual friend at a school function.

She, of course, would have to ask her father's permission. That's the way things were done in the Good Old Days. Permission granted, we took in a movie on a warm June evening.

The hay was ready for its first cutting and our spring calves were rollicking in the meadow. Being farm kids, we spent more time in the months that followed talking across a wooden fence or snapping beans on a porch swing than on "dates." I even spent my fair share of time helping her father put up stacks of hay and oats, but I gained his trust and confidence in the process.

By the time of the last cutting of the summer, I was profoundly in love with that redheaded girl, and I think she was at least somewhat in like with me. We married on the first anniversary of that first date. Janice was 18 and I, 21.

We're still not too sophisticated, my dear wife and I. I'd still rather chew on an oat sprig than just about anything, and she still lets me snap her beans on the old porch swing.

John Slobodnik

$\mathcal{W}$hat is there about a father shaving that fascinates his son? My father always endured me standing, hands on chin, watching him wield the straight razor in front of the kitchen mirror.

That was in the years before we had running water, and Daddy's basin of steaminess was fresh from the tea kettle. It was warm on my face as I watched, spellbound by the manly art of shaving.

Soon after our marriage, Janice bought me a brand-new shaving mug as a birthday gift. Years later, after our son was old enough to understand the differences between his mother and me, I found him intently staring as I shaved. It was a mirror image of Daddy and me, right down to the Burma-Shave shaving soap in the mug. The only thing that had changed was a safety razor for the strop-sharpened straight one.

Like most men today, I have succumbed to an electric contraption to mow down my whiskers. But my mug and brush still sit on a bathroom shelf. You never know when the electricity might fail. Or when I might have an urge to lather up. There would probably be plenty of nicks, but I'll bet Burma-Shave and I could teach a grandson something about shaving back in the Good Old Days.

And maybe he could remind me of the wide-eyed fascination of youth.

$\mathcal{B}$ack in the Good Old Days, there was a lot more to the Fourth of July than fireworks. Patriotism was something that we lived every day of our lives, not just on national holidays.

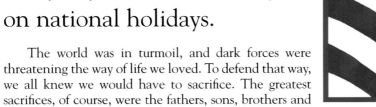

The world was in turmoil, and dark forces were threatening the way of life we loved. To defend that way, we all knew we would have to sacrifice. The greatest sacrifices, of course, were the fathers, sons, brothers and sweethearts whose heroic blood was shed on faraway battlegrounds.

But sacrifice on the home front also made our defense possible. Canned goods were in demand for our fighting forces, so millions of us grew Victory Gardens—food to replace that which was rationed.

Defense plants were manned by women. The younger set gathered recyclable metals to be funneled into the war effort. The few extra dollars we had were turned into War Bonds.

As we locked arms against a common enemy, patriotism was woven into every fiber of life.

Independence Day was so much more than a holiday. It was an outward affirmation of what we lived, what we breathed, what we were.

You'll never fill your basket if you keep eating the berries," Mama chided me one Saturday in early July. "How are we ever going to have enough for my preserves, much less for the strawberry shortcake?"

We were picking in a strawberry patch at a neighboring farm. There was an ice-cream social planned for the following day, and Mama knew that strawberry shortcake with homemade vanilla ice cream was my favorite dessert.

"All right, Mama," I whined, promising to be good. And I was—for a while.

Berry picking can turn into hot, itchy, backbreaking work pretty quickly for a youngster. Never mind my mother's assertion that I was "closer to the fruit." Following her reasoning, it was easier for me to pick berries than from her lofty height.

All of that sweat with none of the instant gratification of sweet, ripe berries being popped into my mouth was more than I could stand. I picked a course that brought me closer to my little sister and her basket. As she bent to pull a juicy fruit from the vine, my hand snaked its way into her cache of berries. My petty larceny would have worked, too, if I hadn't gotten greedy. Three or four berries into the crime, Donna caught movement out of the corner of her eye. "Mama!"

There went *my* strawberry shortcake on Sunday!

The ice-cream social was churning into a roaring success. Fresh cream, sugar, eggs, salt and vanilla extract had already made four or five hand-cranked freezers-ful of the rich, thick dessert. Huge dips decorated the top of the strawberry shortcake.

Ah, the days before we heard about cholesterol—either good or bad!

Our ice-cream turbine was getting hot. Mr. Jones had cranked up a sweat in the torrid July afternoon, mopping his brow with his white handkerchief. It was time for some cool lemonade to repay him for all his hard work.

Of course, all of the ice was designated to join rock salt in the freezer bucket, so there was none to go in the pitcher of lemonade. Still, the fresh-squeezed mixture was wonderfully tart and refreshing in the afternoon heat.

Mr. Jones gratefully pulled a glass from the tray. He drained the first glass without taking a breath and then asked for more. Soon our "turbine" was cranking with renewed gusto and another freezer of winter in July was ready for the table.

$\mathcal{A}$ covered bridge along a country road in late summer was a dream come true for a young couple in the Good Old Days.

The *clip-clop* of a trusty horse's hooves turned hollow on the wooden boards of the bridge, and then the cool well of the bridge beckoned the suitor to reign in long enough to indulge in what we innocently called "spooning."

Summer was the time of blossoming love. The long days of hard work begged for relief in the form of barn dances, parlor parties and box socials. Even into the 1940s, many rural areas still used equine transportation, and a buggy was just the ticket for a date with your best girl.

In those days, country roads were often cooled with an archway of trees; rarely was the arbor cut back like along today's highways. That, like the bridge, shaded the girl and her beau from both the sun and prying eyes.

At the end of the evening, a good horse was given its head and *clip-clopped* its way home, leaving the young couple to revel in the warmth of summer love.

The first flyover of the Canada geese was always a welcome herald to our little farm. It signaled the end of the long summer of back-breaking work.

Whether we were ready for it or not, autumn was on its way. The last loads of winter's supplies were either already in or heading for barn, pantry or root cellar.

The breeze that blew the geese southward was a breath of fresh air at the end of the "dog days" of late summer. It always reminded me of my favorite James Whitcomb Riley poem, *When the Frost Is on the Punkin:*

> *They's something kindo' harty-like about the atmusfere*
> *When the heat of summer's over and the coolin' fall is here—*
> *Of course we miss the flowers, and the blossoms on the trees,*
> *And the mumble of the hummin'-birds and buzzin' of the bees;*
> *But the air's so appetizin'; and the landscape through the haze*
> *Of a crisp and sunny morning of the airly autumn days*
> *Is a pictur' that no painter has the colorin' to mock—*
> *When the frost is on the punkin and the fodder's in the shock.*

As we breathed deeply the first cooling breezes, the geese honked their farewells and the golden-edged leaves waved back. Soon the frost would be on the punkin.

We farm boys reveled in the moment—and then it was back to work.

John Slobodnik

Once the frost was on the pumpkin, it wasn't long until the pumpkin was turned into a jack-o'-lantern.

Halloween was upon us, and every home was illuminated with a grinning ghoul on the front porch beckoning trick-or-treaters.

The pulp had been scraped from the hull through a cap cut in the cranium of the pumpkin. Our favorite autumn treats—pumpkin pie and pumpkin bread—were the fringe benefits to preparing a jack-o'-lantern.

It seemed that every kid's papa or grandpa knew how to transform a pumpkin into a jack-o'-lantern. With surgical precision, he carved eyes, nose and mouth with his trusty Barlow pocketknife. Then he lit a six-inch candle and dripped hot wax in the center of the pumpkin's base and set the candle in the wax to hold it firmly in place.

That night, light danced from our jack-o'-lantern and Mama's homemade treats welcomed witches, ghosts and hobgoblins to our door.

One of my favorite autumn chores was ridding our yard of leaves. The giant oaks and maples that cornered our yard had shaken off their coats of crimson and gold.

What the wind had not carried over the hill was calling for a day of fun. "Fun?" you might ask. Well, to me, leaf raking was more fun than work.

First we gathered them into huge piles, raking sections of the yard like a giant checkerboard. We held races to see who could rake a section the quickest and cleanest. Daddy made sure we were not skipping fencerow or flower bed in our bid to become champion raker of the hilltop.

We were then free for an hour or more to romp in the leaves. We dove headlong into the piles, burrowing like moles through them. Our dog, Frisky, tore through the mounds as we taunted him from the cover. When the piles were scattered, we raked them together and the fun continued.

Lengthening shadows of afternoon led Daddy back to the front yard. Following his lead, we pulled our mounds together and Daddy set the mountain of leaves on fire. Pungent smoke drifted up from the licking flames. Soon our autumn ritual was over. Only the memories—and a few glowing embers—remained.

Thanksgiving was a treasure of time-honored traditions back in the Good Old Days.

Its biggest tradition was the time it gave us to take a break from our workaday lives, gather together as a family and reflect on just how thankful we really should be.

One tradition we shared with a lot of other families was, before asking God's blessing upon the food, we each in turn gave a reason we had to be thankful. It might be as simple as our gratitude for a lost tooth—that, after all, meant a nickel from the tooth fairy. Daddy always completed our circle of gratitude with his profound, traditional reason: "I'm just thankful we're all able to be here together again this year."

We didn't always have a turkey, but when we did, my little sister and I usually got to pull the wishbone—that Y-shaped bone from the breast of the bird. Making a wish first, we pulled until it snapped. The one with the joint part of the bone was sure to get his or her wish.

Another tradition was not so pleasant. Toothpicks held Mama's two-layer cakes together. The first person to find a toothpick had to wash the dishes—and that was a big job! I therefore avoided cake until late in the afternoon.

Whether simple or profound, I will always cherish our Thanksgiving traditions. These days we gather at our house for the holiday. Now I am the one who completes the circle, gratefully saying, "I'm just thankful we're all able to be here together again this year."

Cold nights seemed even colder back in the Good Old Days. For a long time I thought they were literally more frigid, but seasonal temperature averages seem to dispute that.

Since perception is a large part of reality, I *know* in my heart that it *was* colder back then.

Cars were far from airtight, and the wind whistled in from everywhere. Just getting started was often a chore. Antifreeze was invented in the 1920s, but wasn't nearly as reliable as our modern versions. Many a trip on a cold winter morning was preceded by thawing out the radiator with a pan of hot coals from the heating stove.

Our homes were almost never insulated, or poorly insulated at best. Sometimes it was cold enough that the water bucket in the house skimmed with ice overnight. Our wood heater was far from central heat.

It has been said that families were much closer in those days. We had to be, if for no other reason than the sake of body heat. Whether bundled up in the drafty car, gathered for games around the stove in our tiny living room, or sharing a bed with my big brother, we were forced to be a close family.

Sometimes I wonder how such warm memories could come from such cold, cold days.

John Slobodnik

Christmas in the Good Old Days was never complete without caroling. We gathered small groups from church and took our performances to the front yards of homes throughout our neck of the woods.

It Came Upon a Midnight Clear had a very special meaning when sung beneath a canopy of stars, surrounded by a snow-covered landscape. Moonlight on the white blanket and the twinkle of lights and candles in frost-layered windows made the scene almost surreal.

Our favorite homes to visit when we went caroling were those of the elderly. They were a most appreciative audience, even the ones not related to us. Usually we were invited inside for hot chocolate, warming tingling toes and fingers before moving on to the next venue.

I trace my love of singing back to those days of cold noses and warm hearts. Caroling for our neighbors was one way I came to understand the Scripture: "It is more blessed to give than to receive." Christmas in the Good Old Days wouldn't have been the same without it.

$\mathcal{T}$ry as I may, I never was able to stay up to catch Santa Claus on his nocturnal visits on Christmas Eve back when I was a youngster.

Usually I tried to listen intently at the door of my room, hoping to catch the jolly old elf. I always fell asleep before his arrival.

Once I even tried bundling up in a chair in the living room. We always left Santa milk, cookies and a note thanking him for the presents he would leave. After slipping gifts under the tree, Santa sat next to the fire, enjoying the treats we had provided. He then scrawled, "Thank you. Santa" on the bottom of the note before returning to his sleigh.

The reindeer, the gifts, the snack and the departure—surely *something* would awaken me, even if I did fall asleep.

It was Daddy who found me. Maybe those visions of sugarplums dancing in my head had entranced me, but my plan to meet Santa Claus was foiled again. Daddy said he was awakened by noise coming from the living room and had just missed St. Nick himself. I must admit I was beginning to have doubts, and my disappointment was supreme.

But there, at the bottom of our note, was a personal greeting: "The cookies were good, Kenny. Some day, when you're big, we'll get to meet. Love, Santa."

*A*s days lengthen, winter strengthens." It was not hard to understand that old proverb as we passed the winter solstice and moved into the brutally cold month of January.

Mama battled January's bitterness with a dedication to the concept of layering. I started out in longhandles and then heavy shirts and overalls. My feet were tucked in thick cotton socks and, after I put on shoes, Mama made me pull on a pair of Daddy's overshoes that were at least four sizes too big.

Next came my heavy coat—the one Mama made for me herself. She then wound a scarf around my neck and topped me off with a knit hat. Gloves or mittens were the final step. By the time I walked out the door, I wondered which was worse: to risk heat stroke while getting dressed for school or to have the sweat forming on my brow turn to a glaze of ice within a hundred feet of our home.

At school, it took an equal effort to peel the layers off. I wasn't alone, as the closet in the back of the schoolroom attested. Soon a small stream of water from the melting snow we failed to scuff off was trickling across the floor. I prayed that I wouldn't catch cold. If I did, my mother might add an asafetida bag to my layers of protection. The lengthening days and strengthening season were no match for Mama.

$\mathcal{B}$undled as we were against the January weather, the wind still bit into us as we watched a fresh layer of snow fall. How deep had it piled up overnight? It looked like it could be a foot of new snow!

School was cancelled, of course, and we could revel in our day of freedom. What better way to spend it than to take to the hills on anything that could slide?

Sleds were in the highest demand, of course, and the kids who had them also seemed to have the most friends on snow days. But if none of us had a sled in good working order, there was always a cardboard box, a section of corrugated steel roofing or something that could be fashioned into a sliding device.

We even tried tying the hood of an abandoned car to a plowhorse, making a makeshift "sleigh." Do *not* try this at home or anywhere else!

We never considered staying indoors where it was warm. Nothing we could do there could compare to the sheer adventure of a day of sledding, skating and building snow forts. We succumbed only when we could no longer feel toes or fingers.

Why waste a day off of school? Too much time was spent inside already! That was our mantra in the Good Old Days.

John Slobodnik

$\mathcal{E}$ven before the last gasp of winter subsided, it was time to get ready for spring planting. A warm day in February, even if snow still covered the ground, was enough for us to get out the seed catalog and the almanac and start planning corn rows and lettuce beds.

This wasn't a wish list like the one we kids made after poring over the Sears, Roebuck & Co. catalog. The seeds the grown-ups were ordering would sustain us over the next year.

I guess that is the most outstanding attribute of the Good Old Days. Even in the bleak lifelessness of winter, our thoughts were constantly on life. There were plenty of tough times when I was my grandson Daniel's age. Economic depression, war, drought—all seemed to stack the deck against us. But we knew spring would follow winter. And, likewise, we knew the seeds of hope, planted by the sweat of our brow and sustained by the grace of God, would ultimately give us the most precious parts of prosperity: Life, Liberty and Love.

Are the Good Old Days gone? Not as long as families endure. Not as long as love lasts. Not as long as there is a new generation to plead, "Grandpa, tell me 'bout the Good Old Days!"

About the Author

Ken Tate, the editor of *Good Old Days* magazine, was born and reared in the Ozark Mountains of southern Missouri. He and his wife, Janice, live on a 400-acre farm that has been in their family for four generations. Ken and Janice have co-edited *Good Old Days* magazines and books for the past 15 years. Through the magazine, books and his *Looking Back* newsletter, Ken has become one of the most popular nostalgic authors in North America.

About the Artist

John Slobodnik was a young aspiring artist when Ed Kutlowski, founding publisher and editor of *Good Old Days* magazine, first commissioned him to paint covers for the magazine in 1972. With a style reminiscent of Norman Rockwell, John gained national exposure for his graceful, nostalgic work. In all, he completed dozens of paintings for Kutlowski and House of White Birches. Today John paints from his studio in Illinois.

Tell Me 'Bout the Good Old Days

Printed in China

First Printing: 2005

ISBN: 1-59217-083-8

Good Old Days Customer Service:
(800) 829-5865